CRUISE SHIPS

StarVirgo

David L. Williams

Ian Allan PUBLISHING

Front cover: *Paradise*
The *Paradise* on builder's trials in 1998. As the disturbed water reveals, she can virtually 'turn on a sixpence', a testimony to the effectiveness of the Azipod propulsion system fitted to her hull in place of conventional screw propellers and steering gear. *Kvaerner Masa*

Back cover: *Costa Atlantica*
Flagship of Costa Cruises, the *Costa Atlantica*, sporting the instantly recognisable upright yellow funnel which is characteristic of all Costa ships, entered service in July 2000. Her owners are said

to be contemplating even larger cruise ships for the future. *Kvaerner Masa*

Title page: *SuperStar Virgo*
One of a pair of stylish new cruise ships under the Star Cruise houseflag, the *SuperStar Virgo* and her sistership, *SuperStar Leo*, are among the largest passenger vessels serving the Far East cruise circuit. *Bettina Rohbrecht*

This page: *Disney Wonder*
A view of the *Disney Wonder* in Southampton Water, during her one and only visit to the port. *David Reed*

First published 2001

ISBN 0 7110 2801 X

© Ian Allan Publishing Ltd 2001

Published by Ian Allan Publishing

an imprint of Ian Allan Publishing Ltd, Hersham, Surrey KT12 4RG.
Printed by Ian Allan Printing Ltd, Hersham, Surrey KT12 4RG.

Code: 0107/B2

Acknowledgements

In appreciation of the help given to me in support of the preparation of this book, I should like to acknowledge the following companies and individuals:

Alstom — Chantiers de L'Atlantique
Carnival Cruise Line
Celebrity Cruises
Costa Cruises
Cunard Line
Curnow Shipping Company
Holland-America Line
Kvaerner Masa Yards
Meyer Werft (Jos. L. Meyer GmbH)
Norwegian Cruise Line
Fred Olsen Cruise Lines
P&O Cruises
Princess Cruises
David Reed (IoW Branch of the World Ship Society)
Bettina Rohbrecht
Royal Caribbean International
Ian Shiffman
Star Clippers
Star Cruise AS Sendirian Berhad

Bibliography

Hornsby, David, *Ocean Ships* (Ian Allan, 2000)
Ward, Douglas, *Complete Guide to Cruising & Cruise Ships 2001* (Berlitz, 2001)
Sea Lines, the quarterly magazine of the Ocean Liner Society (various issues)
Marine News [quarterly Passenger Ships Updates], the monthly magazine of the World Ship Society (various issues)

Introduction

Since the early 1970s, ocean-cruise holidays have taken off like never before. Today, in excess of eight million persons annually take a cruise somewhere in the world, equating to revenues of more than $50 billion. According to announcements in the late 1990s, cruising has become the fastest-growing sector of the United Kingdom tourist market. At Southampton, the United Kingdom's premier passenger port, this translates into around 150 calls now being made each year by a growing number of cruise ships, representing some 300,000 passenger movements. Between them, the 'Big Eight' cruise operators (Carnival, Royal Caribbean, Star, Princess, Norwegian, Celebrity, Holland-America and Costa) carried a total of 6.5 million passengers in 1999.

To meet this booming demand, orders for new passenger ships stand at an all-time high. In January 2001 there were 51 cruise ships on order, equal to approximately 85,000 additional berths. Of this total, 40 vessels (or just under 80%) have been ordered from just four shipyards (Alstom — Chantiers de L'Atlantique, Fincantieri, Kvaerner Masa and Meyer Werft).

This constitutes an amazing reversal of fortunes for the ocean-going passenger ship, whose very existence, barely a quarter of a century ago, was threatened by the rapidly-expanding passenger aviation industry fuelled by (comparatively) cheap flights.

Cruising has been a feature of passenger-ship operation for well over a century, having developed early on in the era of the ocean liner. Focusing mainly on the wealthy, as an alternative to overland tours, companies like Orient, P&O, Royal Mail and others were offering excursion holidays at sea as long ago as the late 1880s.

Regular-service passenger shipping was, essentially, a seasonal trade, but, as discerning ship-owners perceived the revenue benefits to be gained from this supplementary business, their vessels were invariably diverted to off-peak cruising. And, as the business grew, so ticket prices were moderated to encourage a larger number of would-be travellers from the general public to succumb to the appeal of a cruise holiday.

During the 1930s, and again, for a time, in the 1960s, certain themed cruise experiences were marketed, showing the potential for the cruise to deliver a very specific, exclusive form of holiday for those who required or preferred it. Selective cruise itineraries were arranged to attract particular groups of passengers seeking a distinctive ambience, character or flavour of cruise, or for a clientèle with a shared interest.

Following the decline of the scheduled-service liner, the large ocean-going passenger ship was reborn as a dedicated cruise vessel, designed and operated for that sole purpose. Amazingly, from tentative beginnings it has been the catalyst for a whole new interest in cruising, as reflected by the massive and growing demand for cabin space. With it, in this highly-competitive modern market, have grown expectations for ever-higher shipboard standards — cuisine, accommodation, on-board facilities and entertainment. In this respect, today's cruise ships offer an unrivalled holiday experience. They have the most modern décor, exhibiting all manner of novel features from atriums to shopping malls, from rotating panoramic restaurants to nightclubs and theatres equal to anything available ashore. As important shop-windows for the wider leisure industry, they attract celebrities and upcoming stars to provide the cruise-taker with night-time entertainment that is second to none.

Today's front-line cruise ships now dwarf the passenger liners of yesteryear from which they were derived. As a measure of the buoyant and expanding cruise market, their rate of growth over the past quarter of a century or so is most revealing. By 1984, with the entry into service of the *Royal Princess*, at 44,588 gross tons, the size of the largest purpose-built cruise ship, compared with those in service in the late 1960s, had doubled. In under three years it had virtually doubled again, Royal Caribbean Line's *Sovereign of the Seas* being the first to exceed the size of the largest two remaining former scheduled-service passenger liners, *Norway* (ex-*France*) and *Queen Elizabeth 2*. In 1996 the first dedicated cruise ship of over 100,000 gross tons, the *Carnival Destiny*, was commissioned, but just three years later her record was broken by the *Voyager of the Seas*, some 25% bigger again and currently the world's largest passenger ship. Yet, in less than three years, when Cunard's new *Queen Mary 2* is commissioned, the size of the largest cruise ship will be raised even higher, to over 150,000 gross tons, and, in her case, a new length record will also be set, at 1,132ft (351m)! What is more, the continuing growth of cruise ships, as illustrated here, has as much to do with the provision of greater recreational space for each passenger as with a crude increase of passenger capacity on each vessel.

A significant trend of the cruise industry over the period in which it has blossomed has been the move away from operational management by traditional ship-owners, first to specialist cruise-ship operators and more recently to companies that are predominantly leisure-industry-based. It is true to say, however, that certain traditional passenger shipping firms still figure prominently in the cruise industry, P&O and Holland-America being among the most successful. Cunard Line still has a strong presence, too, although, having lost its independence and subsequently passed through several owners, it is primarily its

name that survives rather than its shipping heritage.

When the cruise industry took off in a big way in the early 1970s, the market-leaders were newly-established operators — some, like Royal Viking Line A/S, having been set up by consortia of long-standing shipping concerns. However, the majority were completely new to the shipping business, some of today's dominant players, such as Carnival and Princess, having emerged in this period.

Today, the trend is increasingly towards the involvement of leisure-industry companies in the running of cruise ships — companies whose backgrounds are in hotel management, entertainment and tourism. Among them are Disney, Seabourn, Radisson, Thomas Cook, Saga, Thomson and Airtours, to name just a few. Considering that the ship itself, in basic terms, is no more than the means of conveyance to a series of pre-selected destinations, and that it is the holiday experience as a whole that is most important, it is evident that businesses whose expertise lies in the successful operation of hotels, theme parks or package holidays have much to offer the modern cruise industry. The balance has certainly shifted from the 'marine' side to the 'hotel' side of the business.

What this means from customers' point of view — 'guests' being the preferred descriptive noun nowadays, rather than 'passengers' — is that the age-old effort to detach the on-board scene from the forces of nature, just a hull's thickness away, almost as a false reality, has been

consciously stepped-up. Equally, just as, in the top hotels around the world, everything functions like clockwork and quality service is provided in a discreet and unobtrusive fashion, so the 'behind the scenes' machinery of the cruise operation is increasingly being concealed from view. No matter how vital the hidden aspects of the operation — laundries, kitchens, shipboard services and so on — may be, their existence has been rather suppressed as the emphasis, at the point of delivery, has been switched to a 'seamless' service in which the results themselves are more important than how they have been achieved.

Moreover, where, in the past, the intrusion of the maritime environment into the day-to-day experience of the passengers was an unwelcome but unavoidable hazard of an ocean voyage, that had to be endured, today any such encroachment is a rare and unfortunate occurrence to be avoided in every possible way. This is reflected in the character of the publicity surrounding the inauguration of new cruise ships, compared to that which, in the past, accompanied the entry into service of new passenger liners. It reinforces the shift of emphasis that has taken place, from a focus on marine power, strength and size to one concerned mainly with guest amenities, passenger space and novel design features. Typically, the commissioning of a liner for the North Atlantic run would have been supported by a plethora of facts and figures illustrating the size and power of her engines, the numbers of rivets used in the construction of her hull and the miles of cables and pipework installed aboard her, and so on. In contrast, the descriptions of new cruise ships, released by the owners' Public Relations departments today, concentrate on the shipboard amenities — the restaurants, theatres, lounges, atriums and shopping facilities, the sizes of the cabins and the number that have private verandahs or balconies, as well as novel features such as casinos and health spas.

Equally, the industry's watchdogs — the consumer organisations, such as Fielding's, Berlitz and Sterns, which monitor cuisine, entertainment and general performance — are no longer interested primarily in punctuality and speed but in the quality of service and the value of the cruise package as an overall holiday experience. Fielding's, for instance, grades all cruise ships according to a 'star' rating system comparable to that used for hotels ashore — grades whose importance is vital to the operating companies and prospective passengers alike. Berlitz rates cruise ships within three broad categories — standard, premium and luxury — by a points system. Points are awarded in each case, out of a maximum of 2,000, for the ship itself and its amenities, the accommodation, the food, the service and the cruise.

Before closing this introduction and looking at the ships themselves and some of the features of their accommodation, mention should be made of the types of cruise ship now operating and the variety of itineraries that are available, for there is a considerable range of choice.

While it would be true to say, as a general statement, that cruises may now be taken just about anywhere in the world, they are in reality concentrated on a number of sea areas. The best-known, of course, are the Caribbean and Mediterranean circuits, while the Pacific coast of North America (including Alaska) ranks as one of the most popular of the new cruise destinations. In recent years the choice has widened further. Star Cruises now offers excursions around the Malaysian peninsula and to islands in the Indonesian archipelago, while Radisson, Renaissance and P&O Holidays make tours around Australasia and out to the Polynesian islands of the central southwest Pacific. Growing interest in cruise holidays in Japan has opened up a cruise circuit in that part of the world, and, half a hemisphere to the east, cruises to the North Cape and the Norwegian fjords remain as inviting as ever. For those who have the staying-power and the essential ingredients of adequate finances and spare time, there are a number of companies making circumnavigations of the globe.

Just as there is great variety in the choice of cruise locations, so too the ships have individual character. Cruises are marketed to suit widely-differing needs, from the boisterous and fun-filled to the contemplative and relaxing. On some ships there is a tradition of formality — routinely dressing for dinner, for example — whereas on others casual attire is the order of the day, every day.

Star Cruises and Holland-America have deliberately sought to re-create the elegant *ambience* of cruising in the past, with stylish but muted décor and furnishings that evoke a bygone era. Disney Cruise Vacations leads the way in the themed-cruise sector, exploiting the iconic imagery of its cartoon characters by linking its cruise trips with stopovers at its theme parks ashore. For those with a more romantic inclination, cruises are available under canvas power aboard a growing number of sailing vessels, affording an unrivalled measure of calmness and serenity. Leaders in this sector of the market are Star Clippers and Windstar Cruises. Last, but most definitely not least, for those with an adventurous spirit, 'explorer' cruises are available from a number of small operators, such as Abercrombie & Kent, Discoverer Reederei and Society Expeditions. Providing accommodation for only a small number of guests, these ships seek out exotic destinations away from the oceans' main highways, at the very fringes of the inhabited world.

Large or small, reflective or lively, ultra-modern or conventionally-appointed, there is something for everybody in the form of the modern cruise holiday. And, having left behind its passenger-liner origins, the purpose-designed cruise ship is definitely here to stay. The challenge for the future will be to develop new concepts and novel attractions for tomorrow's cruise-holidaymakers in satisfaction of customer aspirations that show no sign of abating.

Albatros (1957-   ) Silver Line
(ex-*Dawn Princess*, ex-*Sitmar Fairwind*, ex-*Fairwind*, ex-*Sylvania*)

Berthed on 18 May 2000 in Southampton's Ocean Dock, from where she operated for many years, first as Cunard Line's *Sylvania* on the North Atlantic service and subsequently as Sitmar's *Fairwind* trading to Australia, this is the Vlasov Group's *Albatros*. She is a good example of the older, converted type of cruise ship which provides a 'package-holiday' standard of cruise to satisfy the requirements of those customers who prefer a more modestly-priced cruise experience. British-built and steam-turbine-powered, and operated by Silver Line, the *Albatros* is at present chartered to Phoenix Horizon, a German concern, under a five-year deal. Interestingly, although now approaching 50 years of age, two others of the four ships of her original class are still engaged in active service — the *Ivernia* as the *Fedor Shalyapin* for the Ukraine Government and the *Carinthia* as *China Seas Discovery*, formerly P&O Holidays' *Fair Princess*. *David L. Williams*

Arcadia (1989-   )
P&O Cruises
(ex-*Star Princess*, ex-*Sitmar Fair Majesty*)

Started as the *Sitmar Fair Majesty* for the old-established Sitmar company and launched on 5 March 1988, this ship was renamed *Star Princess* in March 1989 following acquisition of her original owners by P&O. The next eight years were spent serving the American cruise market for Princess Cruises, alternating between base ports at San Francisco, for West Coast itineraries, and Fort Lauderdale, for cruises in the Caribbean. In 1997, she was transferred to P&O to fill the gap left by the old *Canberra* in the United Kingdom cruise market out of Southampton, which is experiencing continuing expansion. Thus, she was renamed a second time, becoming the *Arcadia*, commemorating a passenger liner formerly employed on the Australia run and also based at Southampton until retired in 1979. Her public rooms include the multi-tiered Pacific Restaurant, the informal Conservatory Restaurant on the Lido Deck, and the Palladium Theatre. *Arcadia* has 11 passenger decks and 583 outside cabins. *P&O Cruises*

Aurora (2000-   ) P&O Cruises

The second of two major new cruise ships constructed for the European branch of P&O's cruise operations, the *Aurora* was launched at Meyer Werft, Papenburg, on 3 February 1999, entering service in late spring the following year. She has a tonnage of 76,152 gross and an overall length of 886ft (270m). Along with the similar *Oriana*, her introduction has done much to rebuild Southampton's importance as a major passenger port. Their cruise itineraries take them to the Mediterranean and the Atlantic islands of Madeira and the Canaries, as well as to other destinations further afield. The *Aurora* has two main restaurants — the Alexandria, which features Egyptian themes and designs, and the Medina, in which the décor follows a Moorish flavour. Other public spaces include a theatre, a show lounge, a nightclub and a casino. *Meyer Werft*

Far left: The *Aurora* seen during trials in the North Sea prior to delivery on 15 April 2000. *Meyer Werft*

Above: The *Aurora*'s Riviera Pool and lido area on Deck 7. *Meyer Werft*

Above left: The casino aboard the *Aurora*, called the Monte Carlo, features gaming machines and blackjack and roulette tables. *Meyer Werft*

Left: One of the *Aurora*'s luxury penthouse suites, complete with baby grand piano. *Meyer Werft*

Big Red Boat I (1965-   )
(ex-*Starship Oceanic*, ex-*Royale Oceanic*, ex-*Oceanic*)

Typical of the final generation of scheduled-service passenger liners which found themselves employed making pleasure cruises instead, this ship has enjoyed a long and successful career in this alternative rôle. Now, though, with the financial collapse in September 2000 of Premier Cruises (her most recent owners), her future is in some doubt. Conceived by Home Lines as the *Oceanic* for the emigrant services from Cuxhaven to Montreal, she is one of very few passenger ships still in service which have steam-turbine powerplants. Driving quadruple screws in a configuration which is not ideal for cruise operations, these give a clear indication of her origins. Having entered service on 31 March 1965, for many years she was based in the United States, maintaining an annual programme of cruises from New York to the Bahamas. The unattractive name *Big Red Boat I* was bestowed upon her in 1999 as part of a general renaming exercise involving much of the Premier fleet. A distinctive feature is the retractable 'Magrodome' over the lido on her upper deck — the first marine installation of its kind. The picture shows her in her previous guise as *Starship Oceanic*. *Ian Shiffman*

Black Prince (1966-   )
Fred Olsen Cruise Lines
(ex-*Black Prince/Venus*)

For many years following her inauguration in 1966, this ship alternated between a regular-service passenger route and a programme of short cruises, routinely changing her name each season according to the nature of her employment. Now a dedicated cruise ship based at Dover, the *Black Prince* combines a programme of excursions of mixed duration in European waters with longer voyages to more distant places each spring and autumn. *Fred Olsen Travel*

The Gallery promenade area on the *Black Prince. Fred Olsen Travel*

Black Watch (1972-   )
Fred Olsen Cruise Lines
(ex-*Star Odyssey*, ex-*Westward*,
ex-*Royal Viking Star*)

One of three passenger ships originally
constructed for the Royal Viking Line and
subsequently stretched to their present
size by the Seebeckwerft shipyard in 1982,
the *Black Watch* joined the Olsen fleet in
1996 as the company's largest vessel up to
that date. She is based at Dover, from
where, in conjunction with the *Black
Prince*, she serves the European cruise
trade, sailing to the Norwegian fjords, the
Atlantic isles and circuits in the
Mediterranean, although she is shown here
departing Cape Town. It has been
rumoured that one of her former consorts,
the *Norwegian Star* (ex-*Royal Odyssey*,
ex-*Royal Viking Sea*), may be purchased to
work alongside her. Fred Olsen vessels
score highly in the modestly-priced
Standard cruises category. *Ian Shiffman*

Left: The Orchid Room restaurant on the *Black Watch*. *Fred Olsen Travel*

Right: A typical buffet spread on a Fred Olsen cruise ship. *Fred Olsen Travel*

Carnival Destiny (1996-   )
Carnival Cruise Line

Celebrated as the first passenger ship to exceed 100,000 gross registered tons, the *Carnival Destiny* and her sisters *Carnival Triumph*, *Carnival Victory*, *Carnival Conquest* and *Carnival Glory* (the latter two still under construction) have taken the cruising vessel from the status of 'floating hotel' to 'floating resort'. She has 12 decks, the topmost being higher than the Statue of Liberty. Décor aboard the *Carnival Destiny* is stunning; superb in every way, impressive yet not overpowering. There are two two-deck restaurants, the Galaxy located forward and the Universe located aft. There are three decks of lounges, with the three-level Palladium show lounge being the most distinctive. Centrepiece of the *Carnival Destiny*'s extensive suite of public spaces is the nine-deck atrium, with its glass-domed rotunda ceiling which extends into a broad indoor promenade. Diesel-electric propulsion, driving twin screws, gives a service speed of 18 knots. The 'Carnival Destiny' class represent the culmination of an ambitious investment programme costing $2.1 billion. As part of a follow-on new-building programme, a new class of ship measuring 960ft (293m) in length and measuring 84,000 gross tons will enter service over the next four years, commencing with the *Carnival Spirit* in January 2001. *Bettina Rohrbrecht*

Carnival Victory (2000-   )
Carnival Cruise Line

Sister ship to the *Carnival Destiny*, the
Carnival Victory entered service in August
2000. The picture shows her at Miami, her
home port. *Ian Shiffman*

Caronia (1973-   ) Cunard Line
(ex-*Vistafjord*)

Resurrecting the name of one of the most famous cruise ships ever built, Cunard renamed this former Norwegian America Line ship in memory of its 'Green Goddess', completed back in 1948. She had retained her original name for 16 years after she joined Cunard, not becoming the *Caronia* until 1999 upon completion of an extensive refit. When she was re-christened, the 24,492-gross-ton ship received more than a new identity; apart from the thorough overhaul, which generally upgraded her appointments as befitted the *de luxe* rating of her future cruise programme, she was also repainted in more-traditional Cunard colours. She now offers a worldwide choice of itineraries, each season taking in new and varied destinations. She is stylishly decorated and extremely well appointed, with capacity for a maximum of 732 passengers. Her former fleetmate, the *Sagafjord*, is now operated by Saga Holidays as the *Saga Rose*. The *Caronia* is shown making an evening departure from Southampton on 25 May 2001.
David L. Williams

The *Caronia* (ex-*Vistafjord*) at Cape Town, during one of the first of her cruises under her new identity. *Ian Shiffman*

Century (1995-　) Celebrity Cruises

Far left: The *Century* commenced year-round cruising from Port Everglades with her maiden departure on 20 December 1995. She was the lead ship of a class of three cruise ships, each around 70,000 gross tons in size and built at the Meyer Werft shipyard at Papenburg, Germany. Aboard these magnificent and highly-rated vessels the majority of the passenger cabins are of the outside type with their own balconies. They also have a small number of exceptionally luxurious private suites. Celebrity Cruises is now part of the Royal Caribbean group.
Royal Caribbean International

Left: *Century*'s three-deck Grand Foyer has nine large television screens built into one wall, displaying constantly-changing scenic images.
Royal Caribbean International

Above right: The split-level Grand Restaurant on the *Century* has huge windows overlooking the stern, and an elegant staircase connecting the two levels.
Royal Caribbean International

Right: The theatre, which has a number of side balconies, can seat 1,000 for each performance. *Royal Caribbean International*

Costa Atlantica (2000-   ) Costa Cruises

The *Costa Atlantica* is the latest and largest addition to Costa Cruises' fleet. Built at the Kvaerner Masa shipyard at Turku, Finland, she entered service in the summer of 2000. At 85,700 gross tons and with an overall length of 958ft (292m), she is among the largest and longest cruise ships afloat, providing her guests with a wide range of recreational, entertainment and dining facilities set in stylish Italian-themed surroundings. Costa Cruises is another shipping company with a long heritage extending back to the days of scheduled passenger-liner operations. A sister ship to the *Costa Atlantica* has been ordered from the same Finnish builder, for delivery in spring 2003. *Costa Atlantica* has diesel-electric engines and Azipod propulsion units. *Kvaerner Masa*

The *Costa Atlantica*'s Caruso Theatre and show lounge is three decks high. *Kvaerner Masa*

The atrium on the *Costa Atlantica* has an observation balcony situated at the top. *Kvaerner Masa*

The Tiziano Restaurant has a spiral stairway linking its two levels. *Kvaerner Masa*

Costa Classica (1991-   )
Costa Cruises

In 1998 Costa Cruises announced plans to have the *Costa Classica* and her sistership *Costa Romantica* stretched to increase their occupancy level by 30%, raising their gross tonnage from 52,926 to around 85,000, and their overall length from 731ft (223m) to 878ft (268m). Work on the *Costa Classica* was due to be completed in March 2001 by Cammell Laird, Birkenhead. However, it appeared in early 2001 that the planned enlargement had been cancelled. The *Costa Classica* has four GMT-Sulzer 8ZL405 diesel engines, each of 7,200hp driving twin screws through reduction gears. Her luxurious interiors feature a blend of traditional and contemporary artistic creations, with furnishings and décor in the tradition of Josef Hoffmann, the Thonet brothers, William Morris and other 19th-century designers. *Costa Cruises*

Costa Marina (1969-   )
Costa Cruises
(ex-*Italia*, ex-*Regent Sun*, ex-*Axel Johnson*)

In 1986 the *Costa Marina*, along with the similar *Costa Allegra*, was rebuilt as a passenger ship for Regency Cruises, after 17 years of service as a container ship. The conversion involved extensive modification work, leaving her quite unrecognisable at its conclusion. She passed into Costa ownership in 1990. Smaller of the pair, at 25,441 gross tons and 572ft (174m) overall length, she can now accommodate a maximum of 1,005 passengers. Sailing on Mediterranean cruises in the summer months, she winters in the Caribbean. Costa Cruises is now part of the huge Carnival Corporation. *Bettina Rohbrecht*

Costa Romantica (1993-)
Costa Cruises

Like her consort *Costa Classica*, the *Costa Romantica* is scheduled to be stretched by almost 147ft (45m), increasing her gross tonnage by some 60% and passenger capacity from 1,905 berths to 2,485. The modifications to the two ships would also include enhancements to their power plants and the addition of a third propeller in order to increase their service speed. Reconstruction of the *Costa Romantica* will commence as soon as work on the *Costa Classica* has been completed, if, indeed, the project now proceeds, as statements issued early in 2001 suggested it might not.

Representing the completion of a $1 billion investment programme in fleet expansion and development, the *Costa Romantica* made her maiden voyage from Miami in November 1993. As the focal point of her Grand Lobby, the *Costa Romantica* has a suspended mobile sculpture by Susumu Shingu, named 'The Cloud'. Her 644 staterooms measure an average of 200sq ft (18.5sq m).
Bettina Rohbrecht

Costa Victoria (1996-   )
Costa Cruises

One of a pair of cruise ships ordered from the Bremer Vulkan shipyard, only the 75,166-gross-ton *Costa Victoria* ultimately entered service with Costa Cruises. Arising from bankruptcy of the shipyard, the second, part-built ship, named *Costa Olympia*, was eventually completed as Norwegian Cruise Line's *Norwegian Sky* to a somewhat modified specification. Like those of other Costa vessels, the interiors of the *Costa Victoria* have been designed in a relaxed, classical style. A distinctive feature is her four-deck-high, forward-looking Concorde Plaza observation lounge located at the front of the superstructure. It has a centrally-placed cone-shaped waterfall and is overlooked by pod-like balconies set in the walls. The seven-deck-high atrium has a planetary theme to its design. Public spaces and cabins are relatively spacious, her capacity for a maximum of 2,200 passengers being on the low side for a ship of her size. Her controllable-pitch twin screws are driven by diesel-electric main engines.
Bettina Rohrbrecht

25

Crystal Symphony (1995-   )
Crystal Cruises

The *Crystal Symphony* was ordered as a follow-on consort to the similar-sized *Crystal Harmony*, capitalising on the success of the earlier vessel. They are regarded as the best of the larger, resort-type cruise ship serving the luxury end of the cruise market. Unlike her companion vessel, constructed in Japan, the *Crystal Symphony* was built in a European shipyard — Kvaerner Masa, in Finland; she entered service in the United States cruise market in April 1995. Following experience gained in the operation of the lead ship, some of her public rooms have been repositioned and other enhancements to her amenities have been made. The *Crystal Symphony* has a number of butler-service suites, including two 982sq ft (91sq m) penthouse suites located on Deck 10. The Crystal Cruises programme of excursions includes an annual 96-day world cruise. Typical among other long-distance 20- to 23-day cruises made by this pair are Singapore to Sydney via Bali, Fremantle, Perth and Adelaide, and San Francisco to Sydney via Hawaii, Western Samoa, Fiji and Noumea. Crystal Cruises is a wholly-owned subsidiary of Nippon Yusen Kaisha. *Kvaerner Masa*

Above: The restfully-decorated Palm Court Lounge. *Kvaerner Masa*

Above right: The *Crystal Symphony*'s casino. *Kvaerner Masa*

Right: The elegant reception area on the *Crystal Symphony* features a hand-cut glass waterfall. *Kvaerner Masa*

Dawn Princess (1997-　)
Princess Cruises

The second phase of P&O's major investment programme in new ships for the Princess cruise operation, launched in the late 1980s, comprised four vessels of 77,000 gross tons. The second ship of this quartet was the *Dawn Princess*, commissioned in May 1997. Diesel-electric propulsion, already introduced on previous ships, was again selected for this new class. Almost 60% of the passenger cabins are located on the outside of the hull, overlooking the ocean, the majority of these having private balconies. There is a wide range of public areas for passenger enjoyment, including a 550-seat theatre-cum-show lounge and a 480-seat cabaret lounge. *Princess Cruises*

Disney Wonder (1999-　)
Disney Cruise Vacations

Introduced in August 1999, the *Disney Wonder*, at 83,338 gross tons and 964ft (294m) overall length, is one of the two largest ships ever to operate for a United States' company (albeit flagged in the Bahamas), surpassing by a significant margin the tonnage — if not the length — of the former Atlantic Blue Riband-holder *United States*. The *Disney Wonder* — seen at the Queen Elizabeth II Terminal, Southampton — and her consort, *Disney Magic*, both built in Italy by Fincantieri, are among the most distinctively-styled passenger vessels that have entered service in recent times. Overall décor and *ambience* evoke the age of *grand luxe* at sea, but in a modern (might one say 'theme park') setting, exhibiting many classically-styled design features: sweeping staircases, grand entrances, elegant restaurants and so on. Decoration in Art Deco style is extensive, helping to recreate this atmosphere of the past. Cabins are large and well-appointed, many having their own verandahs. The specially-constructed terminus used by Disney's luxury cruise ships at Port Canaveral is a replica of the old Ocean Terminal at Southampton, opened in July 1950 as the home base for the transatlantic operations of Cunard's *Queen Elizabeth* and *Queen Mary*, but demolished 30 years later. *David Reed*

Elation (1998-   )
Carnival Cruise Line

Penultimate vessel of the eight-ship 'Fantasy' class — probably the most ambitious single new-building project ever conceived in the passenger-shipping business — the *Elation*, like her sisters, was built in Finland at the Kvaerner Masa yard, formerly Wartsila. She was the first cruise ship to be fitted with Azipod propulsion units, driven by the diesel-electric main engines, which pull rather than push the ship through the water. In keeping with the style of this class of ship, aimed at the mass market, she is comfortably appointed, offering a wide range of entertainment, recreational and dining options, though décor is perhaps a tad brash and excessive, as evidenced in the rather lavish multi-tiered show lounge. *Kvaerner Masa*

The six-deck-high atrium aboard the *Elation*, reached from the main entrance on Deck 7, is topped by a glass dome. *Kvaerner Masa*

Enchantment of the Seas
(1997-   )
Royal Caribbean International

Fourth of the 'Legend of the Seas' class or 'Project Vision' series, the *Enchantment of the Seas,* together with her sister ship, *Grandeur of the Seas,* was built by Kvaerner Masa, whereas the other four ships of the group were constructed at St Nazaire by the Chantiers de L'Atlantique yard. The 'Enchantment' pair were the first to break with Royal Caribbean Cruise Lines tradition by having their Viking Crown panoramic lounge placed centrally, separate from the aft-positioned funnel structure, this giving them a sleeker profile. Measuring 74,140 gross tons and 915ft (279m) in length overall, the *Enchantment of the Seas* entered service in July 1997. Comparable in size with Carnival Cruise Line's 'Fantasy' series, the Royal Caribbean ships score consistently higher for shipboard features, food and quality of service. Apart from the Viking Crown lounge, the *Enchantment of the Seas* has a seven-deck-high atrium, a two-tier main dining room and two show lounges. *Bettina Rohbrecht*

Europa (1999-   )
Hapag-Lloyd

Hapag-Lloyd's new, six-star-rated *Europa*, which entered service in September 1999, is rivalled only by the *Crystal Harmony* and *Crystal Symphony* and the ships of Radisson Seven Seas Cruises as one of the top luxury cruise ships afloat. In fact, with a score of 1,855 out of a possible 2,000, according to Berlitz's assessment, she presently ranks as the market leader among the small-to-medium-sized ships. The *Europa*, seen here berthed at Southampton, is diesel-electric-powered, driving twin azimuth propulsion pods to achieve a service speed of 24 knots. Passenger accommodation is all-suite for a maximum of 450 passengers, each suite measuring a minimum of 290sq ft (26.8sq m). Public spaces aboard this intimate vessel include the 446-seat Europa Restaurant, the Grand Lounge, an atrium and the Casino Royal — all beautifully furnished, with a restrained elegance exhibited throughout. There is a discreetly-located deck reserved for those passengers who prefer to sunbathe *au naturel*. *David L. Williams*

Seen entering the Solent as she departs Southampton on 17 August 2000, the *Europa* is the product of the Kvaerner Masa shipyards. She is 28,437 gross tons in size and measures 652ft (199m) in overall length. *David L. Williams*

Explorer of the Seas
(2000-   )
Royal Caribbean International

Currently one of the two largest passenger ships ever built, the *Explorer of the Seas* is the second of Royal Caribbean's 'Project Eagle' class which will ultimately comprise five ships, providing an unrivalled 19,200 passenger berths. The *Explorer of the Seas* measures 137,308 gross tons and 1,020ft (311m) in length overall. The passenger accommodation is superb, comprising premium ocean-view suites or cabins, inside-viewing cabins, standard ocean-view cabins and interior (no-view) cabins. The inside-viewing cabins have bay windows overlooking the horizontal atrium. Most extraordinary among the innovative public rooms and amenities is a regulation-size ice-skating rink which can cater for up to 900 persons. The photographs show the *Explorer of the Seas* from bow quarter and stern quarter as she passes through the Solent in October 2000, inward-bound for Southampton. *(both) David L. Williams*

Above right: The galley which serves the nearby main dining room. *Kvaerner Masa*

Right: One of the atrium lobbies that connect the 394ft (120m) Royal Promenade. The atrium rises through 11 decks. *Kvaerner Masa*

Above right: The *Explorer of the Seas'* three-level main dining room. The levels are connected by a dramatically-styled staircase. *Kvaerner Masa*

Right: The theatre on the *Explorer of the Seas* spans five decks and has 1,350 seats. *Kvaerner Masa*

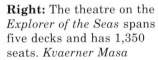

Right: The pool and lido area, forward of the Viking Crown Lounge.

Galaxy (1996-   )
Celebrity Cruises

Celebrity Cruises' Galaxy was delivered in October 1996 as the second of the 'Century'-class ships, entering service two months later. The three vessels of her group were the largest passenger ships constructed in Germany up to that time, Meyer Werft, Papenburg being the builder. The design retains diesel power for its main engines, the machinery having an interesting arrangement comprising two nine-cylinder units linked with two six-cylinder units — the mixed power levels of this configuration permitting greater operational flexibility. Propulsion is by twin controllable-pitch screws. Passengers, normally about 1,900 in number (maximum 2,680), are catered for in comfortable, well-appointed cabins. A combined observation lounge and discothèque, called the Stratosphere, is one of the best of the ship's excellent public rooms. Galaxy has on display a superb collection of reflective artwork depicting life in its many forms, all assembled by Christina Chandris, the wife of the Company Chairman. Celebrity's cruise itineraries alternate between the Latin American or Caribbean circuits in winter and the Mediterranean, the coast of Alaska or the United States' eastern seaboard during the summer months.
Meyer Werft

The *Galaxy*'s cinema doubles as a conference centre catering for corporate and educational gatherings at sea, which are growing in popularity.
Royal Caribbean International

One of the *Galaxy*'s two atriums, the Grand Foyer is four decks high. *Royal Caribbean International*

Grand Princess (1998-)
Princess Cruises

Currently the largest ship in the Princess Cruises fleet, the *Grand Princess* is the lead ship of a class of four giant cruise vessels of over 100,000 gross tons. For a brief period she was the largest passenger ship ever built (an accolade that has now passed, by the slenderest of margins, from the *Voyager of the Seas* to the *Explorer of the Seas*). The *Golden Princess* joined her in April 2001, to be followed by the *Star Princess* in 2002. A fourth vessel, due to enter service in 2003, has yet to be named. Two even larger ships are on order for Princess from the Mitsubishi Heavy Industries shipyard in Japan for delivery in 2003 and 2004. At 108,806 gross tons, with a length overall of 951ft (290m), the *Grand Princess* ranks with the huge cruise ships being introduced by Carnival, Royal Caribbean and Star. *P&O*

Built by Fincantieri, the *Grand Princess* began her inaugural voyage, from Istanbul to Barcelona, on 26 May 1998. She continues to work the Mediterranean cruise circuit, centred on the rugged Amalfi Coast and the Adriatic Sea, transferring to Miami for a programme of winter Caribbean cruise excursions. The *Grand Princess* has a particularly high provision of staterooms of the outside type, 80% of which have private balconies or verandah terraces. Among her numerous comfortable and stylish public areas are a three-deck-high Grand Plaza, a glass-walled nightclub suspended above her stern, a purpose-designed wedding chapel — the first to be provided on an ocean-going cruise ship — and a 'virtual reality' zone! *P&O*

Grandeur of the Seas
(1996-   )
Royal Caribbean International

Grandeur of the Seas, the third of the 'Project Vision' series and the first of the Finnish-built duo from the six-ship class, joined her fleetmates in 1996. Since then she has been employed on Royal Caribbean's broad programme of worldwide excursions. She has twin fixed-pitch screw propellers driven by her diesel-electric main engine plant. Fielding's *Worldwide Cruises* rating system grades the 'Project Vision' group as five-star. Passenger-space ratios (the gross tonnage divided by the number of passengers carried), depending on occupancy levels, average out at 38.5. Compare this photograph with that of the *Splendour of the Seas* on page 74 to get a better impression of the different locations of the Viking Crown lounges in this class. *Bettina Rohbrecht*

The Boutique shopping area on the *Grandeur of the Seas*. *Kvaerner Masa*

Holiday (1985-)
Carnival Cruise Line

Of its class of three similar ships (the others being the *Jubilee* and the *Celebration*), only the *Holiday* was constructed at the Akers shipyard in Denmark — the only large passenger ship of any note to be built in that country. At the time of their completion, the three vessels were among the largest passenger ships ever to be designed specifically for cruising. The *Holiday* entered service on 3 June 1985, based at Miami for Caribbean cruises. She has a tonnage of 46,052 and her overall length is 727ft (222m) — some 10ft (3m) shorter than her Swedish-built consorts. Although she is now 16 years old, her accommodation remains at a high standard, with numerous public rooms distributed on two entertainment decks, flowing out from a long, wide indoor promenade. Her two main dining rooms are the Four Winds and the Seven Seas. *Carnival Corporation*

Horizon (1990-   ) Celebrity Cruises

The *Horizon* was the ship with which Celebrity Cruises established itself as a player in the Alaskan cruise market when she made her first voyage in that region in May 1996. She had been completed six years earlier, in April 1990, being employed initially on the Caribbean circuit, interspersed with cruises to Bermuda. The 46,811-gross-ton, diesel-engined, twin-screw *Horizon* was built at the Meyer Werft shipyard, Papenburg. She is seen here berthed at the Queen Elizabeth II Passenger Terminal at Southampton Docks. *Horizon* generally exhibits contemporary styling, both internally and externally. However, her two-deck-high lobby, with its subtle coral colouring, is reminiscent of the 'Miami Beach Hotel' look of the interwar years. The *Horizon* was extensively refurbished in October 1998. *David Reed*

Infinity (2001-   ) Celebrity Cruises

The second ship of the 'Millennium' class, the *Infinity* is seen completing fitting-out at St Nazaire. These ships, already renowned for their innovative gas turbine-electric main engines and podded propulsion system, are commodiously and elegantly appointed. Cabins are larger than average in size, and the public spaces exhibit a stylish décor and a grandeur commensurate with the status of these front-line ships. Accommodation is provided for just over 2,500 passenger 'guests'. Experience with the lead ship, *Millennium*, revealed problems with the podded propulsion units, necessitating modifications. In the case of *Infinity*, these were incorporated prior to delivery, delaying her inaugural cruise; her rescheduled maiden voyage commenced from Fort Lauderdale (Port Everglades) on 3 March 2001, taking her via the Panama Canal to San Diego. *Alstom — Chantiers de L'Atlantique*

Maasdam (1993-   )
Holland-America Line

The four ships of the 'Statendam' class entered service from 1993, the quartet being completed with the *Veendam* in 1996. Their size statistics are 55,451 gross tonnage and 719ft (219m) overall length. The *Maasdam* was the second to enter service, in December 1993, joining a prestigious cruise fleet renowned for its high standards of comfort, cuisine and service. Holland-America, now part of the Carnival Corporation, tends to aim its cruises towards the higher-grade end of the market. The *Maasdam* has 10 passenger decks. Her public spaces are centred around a three-deck Grand atrium which has a monumental glass sculpture by Luciano Vistosi as its centrepiece. Her $2 million collection of craftworks and artefacts, including treasures dating from the 17th, 18th and 19th centuries, recalls an era of adventure and discovery. *Holland-America Line*

Scene by the pool on the *Maasdam*'s sun deck. *Holland-America Line*

Maxim Gorkiy (1969-)

Government of the Republic of Russia

(ex-*Maksim Gorkiy*, ex-*Hanseatic*, ex-*Hamburg*)

Conceived originally as one of the last regular-service transatlantic passenger liners (though she did not, in fact, perform these duties for any length of time), the *Maxim Gorkiy* is today the flagship of a once-great (but now dwindling) passenger fleet, now owned and operated by the Russian Government and previously known as the Soviet Union's Sovtorgflot. Her greatest claim to fame was when she was used as the location for a summit meeting between US President George Bush and Soviet General Secretary Mikhail Gorbachev, off Malta in November 1989. The *Maxim Gorkiy* continues to operate low-budget cruises on behalf of Phoenix Seereisen, by which she has been chartered long-term since December 1992. Well maintained and regularly refurbished, she is handsome and well-designed but, like other ships constructed primarily for scheduled passenger work, she is now rather dated. *Bettina Rohbrecht*

Majesty of the Seas
(1992-   )
Royal Caribbean International

Completed in April 1992, the *Majesty of the Seas* was the last of three very similar ships built at the Chantiers de L'Atlantique shipyard at St Nazaire, which represented a substantial leap in the size of contemporary cruise ships and hinted at the potential growth offered by this vibrant business. Her sisters are the *Sovereign of the Seas*, commissioned in January 1988, and *Monarch of the Seas*, which entered service in November 1991. These were the first cruise ships to exceed the (then) size of the two largest remaining former passenger liners, the *Norway* (ex-*France*) and the *Queen Elizabeth 2*. (The gross tonnages of the *Norway* and the *Queen Elizabeth 2* have since been increased and are now greater than that of the *Majesty of the Seas*.) *Bettina Rohbrecht*

One of the *Majesty of the Seas'* two restaurants, which have
Hollywood musical themes as the inspiration for their décor.
Each night, diners can enjoy dishes of different national flavours,
the atmosphere on each occasion being complemented by the
waiting staff's dressing in the appropriate costume.
Royal Caribbean International

The five-deck Centrum on the *Majesty of the Seas* — the focal point
of a long atrium lobby which has two glass-walled elevators.
Royal Caribbean International

Mercury (1997-   )
Celebrity Cruises

Last of the 'Century'-class ships completed by Meyer Werft for Celebrity Cruises, the *Mercury* has a capacity for 1,890 passengers on Basis 2 (ie assuming that each cabin is occupied by a maximum of two passengers) in a high grade of luxury and spaciousness. Her gross tonnage is 77,713 and her overall length is 866ft (264m). She entered service in November 1997, following formal acceptance at a ceremony conducted at Eemshaven, Germany, upon the successful completion of her builders' trials. The 'Century'-class ships are powered by geared diesels driving controllable-pitch propellers. They are noted for the stylishness of their interiors, and each has a number of private suites offering an exceptionally high standard of accommodation. The *Mercury* is altogether a stunning ship, inside and out. Among the passenger facilities on board is a three-deck-high atrium positioned aft, a two-tiered main restaurant capable of serving around 1,100 guests at a single sitting, and an observation lounge with seating for 500. The origins of Celebrity Cruises can be traced back to the Chandris Lines, which once operated scheduled services from Europe to Australasia.
Royal Caribbean International

Right: The *Mercury*'s four-deck-high foyer with marble-floored lobby and waterfall. *Royal Caribbean International*

Far right: The Aquaspa, central feature of a health suite comprising a thalasso-therapy pool with active water-jet stations, a room for 'rasul' mud treatment, a sauna and a steam room.
Royal Caribbean International

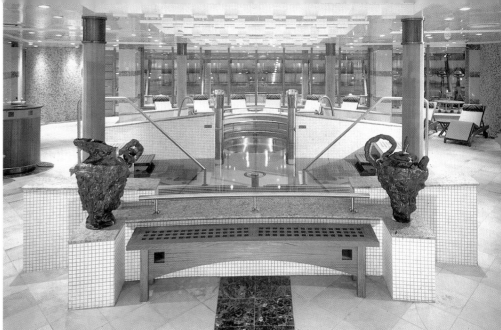

Right: The split-level Manhattan Restaurant, located at the *Mercury*'s stern, provides sea views through large picture windows. Michelin chef Michel Roux is Director of Cuisine for Celebrity Cruises. *Royal Caribbean International*

Millennium (2000-   )
Celebrity Cruises

The aptly-named 'Millennium' class, the name-ship of which entered service in June 2000, are the first large passenger ships to be fitted with gas turbine-powered electric-drive engines. Besides this, as another innovation with this class, the *Millennium* is also celebrated as the first vessel to be fitted with so-called 'Mermaid' pods — French/Swedish-designed multi-directional propulsion units which take the place of conventional screw propellers. Royal Caribbean International, owner of Celebrity Cruises, first hinted at such radical developments in powerplants and propulsion systems in April 1998, around the time the first orders were placed. Though gas turbine-electric-drive installations result in higher fuel costs, this is more than offset by reductions in engine-room manning levels, besides which space otherwise occupied by machinery is released for additional passenger accommodation. Similarly, the 'Mermaid' pods, which are attached as appendages to the underwater hull, obviate the need for normal steering gear. Built by Chantiers de L'Atlantique at St Nazaire, in the same building dock as the *France* (now *Norway*), the *Millennium* measures just over 91,000

tons gross and 964ft (294m) in length overall. Following the *Infinity* (the second of the class), a further three ships of this type are on order due to enter service between 2002 and 2004. A novel feature of the *Millennium* — though some may shudder at the prospect — is a 14,000sq ft (1,300sq m) shopping arcade. *Alstom — Chantiers de L'Atlantique*

Below: The two 'Mermaid' pod installations attached to the *Millennium*'s hull.
Alstom — Chantiers de L'Atlantique

Right: The enclosed hydropool, one of the features of the *Millennium*'s Aqua Spa complex. The main, outdoor pool, the Malibu, is located on the top deck.
Alstom — Chantiers de L'Atlantique

Below right: A quiet corner of the Olympic Restaurant, named after the White Star liner of that name and featuring original decorated walnut wood panelling in Louis XV style, taken from the *Olympic*'s *à la carte* restaurant. *Alstom — Chantiers de L'Atlantique*

Monarch of the Seas
(1991-   )
Royal Caribbean International

Second of Royal Caribbean's 70,000-gross-ton, diesel-engined giant cruise ships, the *Monarch of the Seas* entered service in November 1991. As this view clearly shows, the prominent Viking Crown lounge, built around her funnel, is a distinctive feature readily distinguishing Royal Caribbean vessels. Following a grounding incident in December 1998 she received an extensive overhaul, during which her passenger amenities were enhanced.
Bettina Rohbrecht

Norway (1961-)
Norwegian Cruise Line
(ex-*France*)

Constructed as the *France* for the Compagnie Générale Transatlantique (French Line), the *Norway* was one of the last superliners to be designed and constructed specifically for the North Atlantic scheduled passenger service. Conversion into a cruise ship has sustained the life of this elegant vessel, making her unique among passenger ships on the contemporary scene. She retains many of the characteristics of her line-voyage days; these include some of her magnificent interior design features, now adapted through the adoption of a modern, 'warm climate' style of décor, as well as her steam-turbine main engines, although the original quadruple screws have now been reduced to just two. Despite her origins, she is now every inch a well-appointed luxury cruise ship, but with that little something extra. A series of major overhauls and renovations have dramatically changed her appearance and her gross tonnage is now 76,049. The regular programme of overhauls has also ensured that she continues to satisfy even the most recent SOLAS (Safety of Life at Sea) regulations. The *Norway* remains (for now, at least) the longest ocean passenger ship ever built, with an overall length of 1,035ft (316m). As a cruise ship she has served as a ferry to her owner's private tropical island in the Caymans, as well as operating more-typical itineraries of long and short duration in the Caribbean and Mediterranean. From the autumn of 2001 she will take up position in the Far East, providing, for the first time, cruises to Asiatic and Pacific destinations. With the appeal of her size and heritage, she remains a favourite even though her dimensions prevent her from passing through the Panama Canal and from docking at the majority of destinations on the various cruise circuits.

Bettina Rohbrecht

Norwegian Dream (1992-   )
Norwegian Cruise Line
(ex-*Dreamward*)

The sister ships *Norwegian Dream* and *Norwegian Wind* entered service in November 1992 and April 1993 as the *Dreamward* and *Windward* respectively, the latter christened at Los Angeles by Barbara Bush, the wife of former US President George Bush. Originally measuring around 39,000 gross tons, both ships were subsequently lengthened by the Lloyd Werft shipyard, commencing with the *Windward* in October 1997, the *Dreamward* following in March 1998. The ships were renamed on their return to service. The modifications increased their capacity from 1,750 to 2,100 berths; gross tonnage is now 50,760, and length overall is 754ft (230m). Offering affordable cruises with that little bit extra, the two ships are known best for their tours to Alaska from Vancouver, via the Inside Passage to Glacier Bay; also to Hawaii, South America and Bermuda. Their diesel engines have a total output of 24,782hp (18,480kW), giving a service speed of 21 knots. *Bettina Rohbrecht*

Norwegian Sky (1999-   )
Norwegian Cruise Line
(ex-*Costa Olympia*)

The diesel-electric, 77,104-gross-ton *Norwegian Sky* is the largest vessel in the Norwegian Cruise Line fleet, although at an overall length of 853ft she is considerably shorter than the *Norway*. She started life as part of a two-ship order for Costa Cruise Line, the first vessel, *Costa Victoria*, being completed and delivered as intended. The second ship, *Costa Olympia*, was barely half-complete

when builders Bremer Vulkan were declared bankrupt and work on the ship was suspended. The partly-built hull was purchased by Norwegian Cruise Line in 1997 for completion by Lloyd Werft as the *Norwegian Sky*. Lloyd Werft has since been contracted to build a second, near-identical ship for Norwegian Cruise Line. Named *Norwegian Sun*, she is due to enter service in August 2001. Norwegian Cruise Line is now a subsidiary company of the Star Cruise AS Sendirian Berhad of Malaya. The photograph shows the *Norwegian Sky*'s upper deck forward of the funnel.
Norwegian Cruise Line

The atrium on the *Norwegian Sky*. Other interior spaces are her two main restaurants, the Four Seasons and the Seven Seas, and a 1,000-seat show lounge. The ship is currently based at Seattle.
Norwegian Cruise Line

Ocean Princess (1999-   )
Princess Cruises

The *Ocean Princess*, the last of a group of four large cruise ships (the other three being the *Sun Princess*, *Dawn Princess* and *Sea Princess*), entered service in February 2000. With her sisters she cruises in the Caribbean until the early summer, when she transfers to Alaskan waters, based either in California or at Vancouver where she is pictured. Passenger capacity is 2,200; gross tonnage is 77,441 and overall length 856ft (261m). The *Ocean Princess* has two main restaurants, the Sardinian and the Tuscan. Like those on many other cruise ships these days, both are non-smoking. There are also two principal lounge areas — a theatre-style show lounge and cinema, and a cabaret lounge with its own bar. Despite her considerable size, the *Ocean Princess* has an intimate feel, with a style of décor which is warm and welcoming — bright but not overpowering. *Ian Shiffman*

Oriana (1995-) P&O Cruises

Just three years after her keel was laid, the *Oriana* was christened by HM Queen Elizabeth at Southampton on 6 April 1995, reviving the name of a well-regarded predecessor which had retired just nine years earlier. The first new P&O passenger ship for 30 years, the *Oriana* was built by Meyer Werft at Papenburg, her access to the open sea involving, as it has for many other large cruise ships constructed at this German yard, a careful tow down the narrow River Ems to Emden. Her maiden cruise of 14 days' duration took her to Madeira, the Canary Islands, Morocco, Gibraltar and Portugal. Since then she has continued to make European cruises from her home port of

Southampton. Elegant and tastefully-decorated, she combines modern and traditional features to provide the best of cruising today with a hint of the style and feel of ocean travel in bygone days. Among the notable attributes of her public spaces, the focal point of her atrium reception area is a four-deck-high waterfall. Along with the *Arcadia*, the *Oriana* operates 'cruise and stay and fly home' holidays. *P&O Cruises*

Above: Making an evening departure from Southampton, the *Oriana* is seen from the Town Quay. She has two acres of deck space, with a broad promenade encircling the ship. There are two restaurants, the Peninsular and the Oriental, the latter overlooking the stern. Other public rooms include the Theatre Royal, Chaplin's Cinema, the Pacific show lounge and — reminiscent of the old *Canberra* — the Lords Tavern Lounge, complete with cricketing mementos. *David L. Williams*

Paradise (1998-)
Carnival Cruise Line

Together, the eight ships of the 'Fantasy' class represent a greater tonnage than the combined tonnages of all the giant passenger liners introduced by all operators on the North Atlantic run between the two World Wars. Last of the series, the 70,637-gross-ton *Paradise* entered service in November 1998. Like her predecessor, the *Elation*, she has azimuth pods driven by her diesel-electric main engines in place of conventional screw propellers, giving improved manœuvrability. The internal layouts of the eight 'Fantasy' ships are identical. Thus, like her consorts, *Paradise* features a rather bold and strident décor, suiting the boisterous, lively type of cruise marketed by Carnival. A quartet of even larger, 84,000-gross-ton ships, measuring 960ft (293m) in length, is set to follow the 'Fantasy' class; the first two, *Carnival Spirit* and *Carnival Pride*, are scheduled to enter service in 2001. *Kvaerner Masa*

Right: The atrium aboard the *Paradise* is linked to a double-width boulevard, from which extend all the principal public rooms. *Kvaerner Masa*

Far right: One of the *Paradise's* spectacular, multi-level lounges. *Kvaerner Masa*

Queen Elizabeth 2 (1969-   )
Cunard Line

Though conceived as a dual-rôle ship, to maintain a limited scheduled service on the North Atlantic for part of the year, the *Queen Elizabeth 2* has functioned essentially as a full-time cruise ship since the late 1970s. Although she continues to make a series of passages from Southampton to New York each season, each one-way voyage may be considered as a luxury cruise in itself, being invariably linked with a return crossing by aircraft. The famous *Queen Elizabeth 2* / Concorde round-trip programme operated in conjunction with British Airways has, however, been suspended since the air crash at Paris in September 2000. Her itinerary of excursions still includes an annual round-the-world cruise. Between October 1986 and April 1987 she was re-engined with a diesel-electric powerplant, simultaneously receiving a major overhaul and renovation of her interiors. She is pictured arriving in Cape Town on a voyage from Southampton in November 2000. *Ian Shiffman*

Now measuring 70,327 gross tons, the 963ft (294m) *Queen Elizabeth 2*, a true ocean liner, remains the flagship of the British Merchant Marine, trading on her superliner status to satisfy a niche market for which big-ship splendour is an important ingredient of the cruise experience. Cunard has ordered a new giant cruise ship which will enter service in 2003, hopefully acting as consort to the *Queen Elizabeth 2*. Already named *Queen Mary 2*, the new liner is set to be a record-breaker, with a gross tonnage of 150,000 and overall length of 1,132ft (345m). The photograph shows the *Queen Elizabeth 2* berthed at her home port of Southampton. *David Reed*

R One (1998-)
Renaissance Cruises

The first of eight (so far) virtually-identical cruise ships built by Chantiers de L'Atlantique, each of 30,277 gross tons and measuring 594ft (181m) in overall length, this is Renaissance Cruises' *R One*. The latest of the series, the *R Eight*, entered service in March 2001 with a preliminary call at Southampton. Diesel-powered, with twin controllable-pitch propellers, these ships serve the Premium cruise market, each accommodating a maximum of 824 passengers. *R One* and *R Two* cruise in the Mediterranean, while *R Three* and *R Four* serve French Polynesia, based at Tahiti; *R Five* operates European cruises, *R Six* serves the Baltic, *R Seven* supports a Caribbean cruise programme and the new *R Eight* will commence a cruise itinerary in southeast Asia — a truly worldwide operation! *Bettina Rohrbrecht*

Radiance of the Seas
(2001-   )
Royal Caribbean International

One of the latest cruise ships to enter service, Royal Caribbean's 88,000-gross-ton *Radiance of the Seas* was commissioned in February 2001 as the lead ship of a new class, the 'Project Vantage' series. The second ship, the *Brilliance of the Seas*, is scheduled for completion in June 2002. The 962ft (294m) *Radiance of the Seas* introduces a number of novel design and engineering features. The profile of the passenger decks incorporates external bays on both sides — one utilised for the verandahs of a number of suites, the other as a panoramic elevator tube extending through five decks and providing open views over the ocean. Dubbed the first 'green' ship because environmental impact has been reduced in every way possible, her main engines are a mixture of gas and steam turbine-electric, with the electric-drive motors located within the underwater casing of the podded propulsion units. The steam turbine unit utilises the waste heat of the two gas turbines to generate electricity as a back-up to the propulsion system and for the hotel services on board. The public rooms on the *Radiance of the Seas* include the Cascades Restaurant, seating 1,104 passenger guests, a three-level 874-seat show lounge and a large cabaret lounge. There is a Centrum, of course, extending through nine decks and connecting with a number of the main public areas. *Meyer Werft*

Radisson Diamond
(1992-   )
Radisson Seven Seas Cruises

To date the only cruise ship of its type, the *Radisson Diamond* is a SWATH (Small Waterplane Area Twin Hull) vessel — in effect, a catamaran. She was completed in 1992 for the Diamond Cruise Line, which has since been restyled Radisson Seven Seas Cruises. Built by Rauma Yards in Finland, she entered service on 30 April 1992, cruising in the Caribbean and the Panama Canal area in winter and working the European circuit in summer. The radically-different shape of her SWATH configuration is reflected in the *Radisson Diamond*'s dimensions. She is 423ft (129m) in overall length and 105ft (32m) across the beam; gross tonnage is 20,295. The *Radisson Diamond* has a small passenger capacity, providing accommodation for only 354. However, her passenger-space ratio is very high, at 57.3, befitting a vessel that offers, along with her fleetmates, a very high standard of luxury, commodiousness and quality of service. Propulsion is by twin nozzles, her slow service speed of 12.5 knots being, perhaps, her only serious weakness, realistically suiting leisurely inter-island cruising rather than long-distance excursions. *David Reed*

Regal Princess (1991-)
Princess Cruises

Sister ship to the *Crown Princess*, at one time the largest ship in either the Princess or the combined P&O/Princess fleets, the *Regal Princess* entered service in August 1991. Originally ordered by Sitmar Cruises, both ships passed to Princess after P&O acquired the Italian concern and its vessels in 1988. The *Regal Princess* (seen here departing Vancouver) and her sister now operate year-round in the Caribbean, based in Miami. Built by Fincantieri, the *Regal Princess* has a gross tonnage of 69,845 and an overall length of 804ft (245m). An extensive refit has added a Lido Restaurant as well as re-modelling her elegant three-deck atrium and the main restaurant. She has an observation dome located above the navigation bridge, incorporating a casino and a lounge with dance floor. *Ian Shiffman*

Rhapsody of the Seas (1997-   )
Royal Caribbean International

Penultimate ship of the six-unit 'Legend of the Seas' class or 'Project Vision' series, the *Rhapsody of the Seas* entered service in May 1997, to be followed a year later by the *Vision of the Seas*. Gross tonnage is 78,491, with principal dimensions of 915ft (279m) length overall and 105ft (32m) beam. Passenger accommodation consists of 2,416 berths.
Royal Caribbean International

The Broadway Melodies Theatre on the *Rhapsody of the Seas*.
Royal Caribbean International

The two-level Edelweiss Restaurant is the *Rhapsody of the Seas'* main dining area; she also has a number of other intimate and informal eating areas. *Royal Caribbean International*

The Solarium has an Olympian look and feel to it. *Royal Caribbean International*

Rotterdam (1997-   )
Holland-America Line

Holland-America Line's new diesel-electric-powered *Rotterdam* entered service in December 1997, belatedly celebrating her owner's 125th anniversary as a major passenger shipping company. Its acclaim as a provider of top-grade cruises over the last 40 years was preceded by a long history of equally-impeccable service on the North Atlantic run from Rotterdam to New York. Along with her consort *Amsterdam*, which joined her in October 2000, the *Rotterdam* is a deeper-draught vessel, better suited for longer-distance cruises in open seas. Likewise, she is capable of 25 knots service speed, suiting longer-distance excursions. Though categorised as offering Premium-rated cruises, these two Holland-America ships are realistically placed at the top end of that band, their accommodation exhibiting a muted splendour reminiscent

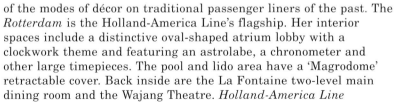

of the modes of décor on traditional passenger liners of the past. The *Rotterdam* is the Holland-America Line's flagship. Her interior spaces include a distinctive oval-shaped atrium lobby with a clockwork theme and featuring an astrolabe, a chronometer and other large timepieces. The pool and lido area have a 'Magrodome' retractable cover. Back inside are the La Fontaine two-level main dining room and the Wajang Theatre. *Holland-America Line*

Above: The *Rotterdam*'s Crow's Nest lounge is a Holland-America feature which can be found on other ships of the fleet. *Holland-America Line*

Above right: The art gallery on the *Rotterdam*'s upper promenade deck displays an impressive array of neo-classical Dutch and Japanese artefacts, sculptures and paintings from the 17th century. *Holland-America Line*

Right: The *Rotterdam*'s informal Lido Restaurant, located by the main pool. *Holland-America Line*

Royal Clipper (2000-)
Star Clipper Cruises

Started at a Gdansk shipyard and completed by De Merwede in the Netherlands, the five-masted *Royal Clipper* is presently the largest fully square-rigged sailing cruise ship, and is styled on the famous German windjammer *Preussen*, built in 1902. She makes an impressive sight under full sail, with a total sail area of 56,000sq ft (5,205sq m) with all 42 sails set. Auxiliary power is supplied by diesel engines driving a single screw. Despite an outward appearance that suggests capstans and windlasses and sea shanties, as part of a rugged sea-going experience, the *Royal Clipper* in fact brings luxury cruising to this type of vessel. Passenger capacity is for 250 in eight grades of accommodation, ranging from two luxury owners' suites and 14 *de luxe* suites to six inside double cabins which have no view. *Star Clipper Cruises*

The *Royal Clipper* has a three-deck-high atrium, containing the main dining room, set immediately beneath one of three swimming pools, which allows natural light into this below-decks area. She has a gross tonnage of 5,051, with an overall length of 440ft (134m). Another novel public area, complementing the relaxed cruising style which characterises a voyage on this sailing ship, is her below-decks Captain Nemo Club lounge, where guests can view the sealife, floodlit at night, through large glass portholes. The *Royal Clipper* is based at Barbados during the winter, cruising to the Grenadines and Windward Islands. In the summer she is based at Cannes, making Mediterranean cruises. *Star Clipper Cruises*

Royal Princess (1984-   )
Princess Cruises

As evidence of P&O's positive intentions for the future of Princess Cruises, the rakish *Royal Princess* represented a major advance when commissioned in November 1984, being almost twice the size of the previous generation of cruise vessels of the 'Love Boat' series. At 45,588 gross tons, and 756ft (231m) in overall length, she was able, briefly, to claim the distinction of being the largest purpose-built cruise ship. Her accommodation is first-rate, representing at the time a key milestone in the overall enhancement of shipboard standards. The central atrium — now a mandatory feature of the modern cruise ship, demanding the most inventive thinking from interior designers — was first introduced aboard the *Royal Princess*. Hers was the creation of the Norwegian naval architect Njal Eide. Her other public rooms are large, spacious and beautifully appointed. The *Royal Princess*, shown berthed at Miami, alternates between the Caribbean and Alaskan cruise circuits, according to the season. *P&O*

Ryndam (1994-)
Holland-America Line

The third ship of the 'Statendam' class, the *Ryndam* was introduced in November 1994. In total, the four ships of her group, all built at Monfalcone in Italy by Fincantieri, left Holland-America with very little change out of $1 billion, constituting a major investment that lifted the company into the upper echelon of cruise-ship operators. A distinctive feature of the *Ryndam* is an array of paintings and other artwork displayed throughout the ship, chronicling the heritage of Holland-America and its Dutch origins. She has a two-deck main dining room with panoramic views on three sides, five lounges, two swimming pools (one covered by an hydraulically-operated glass 'Magrodome'), a library and a casino. The 'Statendam'-class vessels are diesel-electric, twin-screw ships designed primarily for sheltered-waters operation. The *Ryndam* is based at Port Everglades. *Holland-America Line*

Seabourn Spirit (1989-   )
Seabourn Cruises

One of a group of three similar ships, the *Seabourn Spirit*, which entered service in November 1989, is an intimate, highly-luxurious small cruise ship catering for just 200 passengers in exceptionally stylish surroundings. At 9,975 gross tons, she measures 440ft (134m) in length. Her consorts are *Seabourn Legend*, completed in March 1992 and refurbished in July 1996, and *Seabourn Pride*, which was commissioned in December 1988. Their yacht-like external appearance is complemented by lavishly-appointed accommodation, with plenty of marble, fine woods and cut glass in evidence. The public rooms, some reached through a wide central passageway, include a compact main cabaret lounge, a nightclub, an observation lounge and a casino. Seabourn also operates the smaller, more select *Seabourn Goddess I* and *Seabourn Goddess II*, as well as the significantly larger *Seabourn Sun*. All are rated highly in the Luxury sector of the cruise market, being five-star-graded, with generous passenger-space ratios. *Bettina Rohrbrecht*

Sovereign of the Seas
(1987-   )
Royal Caribbean International

The *Sovereign of the Seas* was the lead ship of a trio of 70,000-gross-ton cruise ships built for Royal Caribbean from the late 1980s which, at the time, were the largest passenger ships in the world. At 73,192 gross tons, and 880ft (268m) long, at a stroke she increased the size of the largest cruise ships by some 30% on entering service in January 1988. She was extensively refurbished during the 1997 season, increasing her capacity to 2,700 berths and enhancing some of her passenger amenities. Unlike the similar-sized vessels of the later 'Project Vision' series, which have diesel-electric powerplants, the *Sovereign of the Seas* and her sisters are geared motorships with controllable-pitch screw propellers. The *Sovereign of the Seas* makes year-round three- or four-night mini-cruises from Miami to the Bahamas. Her friendly crew are mainly of Caribbean extraction.
Royal Caribbean International

The Gigi dining room, one of two main restaurants on the *Sovereign of the Seas*. *Royal Caribbean International*

The *Sovereign of the Seas*' cinema. *Royal Caribbean International*

Splendour of the Seas
(1996-   )
Royal Caribbean International

Second of the 'Project Vision' or 'Legend of the Seas' class (a development of the company's first three 70,000-gross-ton vessels), this is the 69,490-gross-ton *Splendour of the Seas*. This class in fact comprises three pairs having similar characteristics as well as distinct differences. Thus, the first two, the *Splendour of the Seas* and the *Legend of the Seas*, built in France at St Nazaire, featured the original concept of near-amidships funnel, with the Royal Caribbean Cruise Line's hallmark Viking Crown panoramic lounge attached to the funnel structure. They are the smallest pair of the six. As a recognition-point, comparison with the *Sovereign of the Seas* reveals that the Viking Crown of the original class of 70,000-gross-ton Royal Caribbean ships actually encircled the funnel, whereas on the *Splendour* and *Legend* it projects forward from the front of the funnel. The next four ships were built to a further-modified design: their funnels were placed aft, and the Viking Crown lounge is a detached structure placed centrally on the upper deck. Glass has been used extensively in this class of ship, allowing unhindered daylight into central areas and clear, free observation of the seascape from most public areas. Another distinctive feature is a seven-deck-high atrium with a parabolic glass ceiling.

Access between decks is by means of exposed lifts which travel up and down the sides of the atrium.
Royal Caribbean International

Above: A detail of the two-deck-high King & I Restaurant, with Siamese decorations and furnishings.
Royal Caribbean International

The *Splendour of the Seas*' seven-deck-high atrium provides links, via glass-sided elevators, to the Viking Crown Lounge.
Royal Caribbean International

A feature of recent Royal Caribbean ships, the stylish solarium on the *Splendour of the Seas*. *Royal Caribbean International*

St Helena (1990-   )
Curnow Shipping Co

Essentially a scheduled-service cargo/passenger liner — one of the very few remaining in operation — the *St Helena* makes regular sailings carrying passengers and delivering mail and provisions to the islands of St Helena, Ascension and Tristan da Cunha on a route which terminates at Cape Town and includes calls, out and back, at Tenerife. Because the accommodation, for just 132 passengers, is not always taken by persons travelling specifically to these destinations, it is also offered for cruise vacations of either long duration — a complete one-way voyage or round trip — or for shorter excursions between intermediate ports of call. Befitting a small vessel with fundamentally a working rota, public spaces on the *St Helena* are limited, but the cabin accommodation is generally comfortable and pleasing. Meals are simple but appetising, and the cruise experience overall is one of extreme relaxation, evoking sea voyages of yesteryear. Even so, the *St Helena* is fully stabilised and air-conditioned, and even has a small pool, providing relief from the heat of the tropics. *Curnow Shipping Co*

One of the comfortable, unostentatious cabins available on the *St Helena*. Her home port is Cardiff. *Curnow Shipping Co*

Star Flyer (1991-   ) and *Star Clipper* (1992-   )
Star Clipper Cruises

Purpose-built for sail cruising along traditional sailing-ship lines, the 3,025-gross-ton *Star Flyer* and *Star Clipper* entered service in July 1991 and May 1992 respectively. Barquentine-rigged, these 366ft (112m) true sailing vessels project the Star Clipper Cruises promotional ethos of combining the character and flavour of a

voyage at sea, experiencing the full sensation of the elements in clipper-ship style, with comfortable and elegant accommodation and 'big ship' dining and entertainment facilities. The emphasis within this framework is on carefree relaxation, and cruising on these vessels is far removed from the hustle and bustle of the larger, conventionally-powered cruise ships. *Star Clipper Cruises*

Another view of the *Star Clipper*. Both the *Star Clipper* and *Star Flyer* are air-conditioned, but, as might be expected, there are fewer public rooms aboard them and they are of a more compact size, although maximum capacity is for only 180 passengers. For the guests' pleasure there is an attractive dining room which has a pronounced nautical decorative finish of polished wood and brass. There is also a bar, a small lounge and a pool.
Star Clipper Cruises

Statendam (1993-)
Holland-America Line

The *Statendam* was the lead vessel of a series of four attractive ships of moderate size that perpetuate the tradition of quality and elegance that has made Holland-America one of the highest-rated of today's larger cruise fleets. Measuring 55,451 gross tons, she entered service in January 1993. Accommodation is provided for 1,266 passengers on Basis 2 capacity (two-person occupancy of all staterooms) or 1,629 maximum (with all available berths occupied). As precursors to the larger 'Volendam' and 'Rotterdam' classes, the 'Statendam' quartet were Holland-America's third generation of purpose-built cruise vessels, following on from the small *Prinsendam* and the later *Nieuw Amsterdam* and *Noordam*. Like her sisters, the *Statendam* has a typical range of excellent public rooms and restaurants radiating from her atrium foyer, with its grand centrepiece sculpture. *Holland-America Line*

The *Statendam*'s spectacular Van Gogh show lounge. *Holland-America Line*

Sun Princess
(1995-   )
Princess Cruises

Princess Cruises' *Sun Princess* was the lead ship in the second phase of P&O's massive regeneration programme for Princess Cruises, launched just over a decade ago, which resulted in four larger and improved vessels based on the 'Crown Princess' type. For a very brief period (barely a year) after entering service in December 1995, the *Sun Princess* was the world's largest cruise ship. Recognising that passenger aspirations were to have more and larger outside cabins with private balconies, the design of the 'Sun Princess' class provides over 40% of the accommodation in this form, with a further 20% lacking balconies but still located on the outside of the hull. The *Sun Princess* has a spectacular four-deck-high atrium with glass lifts, a waterfall and full-size palm trees, lending a sense of space and brightness to her interiors. The Princess Theatre show lounge/cinema seats 550, while a separate cabaret lounge with its own bar can accommodate 480. *P&O*

SuperStar Aries
(1982-   )
Star Cruises
(ex-*SuperStar Europa*, ex-*Europa*)

The former Hapag-Lloyd cruise ship *Europa*, built in Germany by Bremer Vulkan, is now one of the leading vessels of the Star Cruises fleet as the *SuperStar Aries*. Having already had a major overhaul in 1995, she was fully refurbished again in 1999 after her change of ownership. Her accommodation layout reflects the thinking of the early 1980s, when vertical division was the vogue, placing cabins in the forward part of the ship, at a distance from engine noise and vibration, with the public rooms placed aft on the same decks. Today's trend is for horizontal division of the public areas, with entire decks generally given over either to state rooms or to passenger amenities. Star Cruises' holidays are relaxed and casual, with friendly Asiatic crews ensuring hospitable and attentive passenger care. The main public spaces on the 37,012-gross-ton, 655ft (200m) *SuperStar Aries* are her Grand Restaurant, overlooking the ocean on two sides, and her stylish theatre/show lounge. *SuperStar Aries* is based at Laem Chabang, the port of Pattaya, Thailand, operating short cruises along the Thailand and Vietnam coastlines, with options for combined resort stayovers. *Star Cruises*

The Lido Bar and swimming pool on the *SuperStar Aries*' Clipper Terrace. *Star Cruises*

The *SuperStar Aries*' Europa Lounge — a reference to her former identity. *Star Cruises*

SuperStar Leo (1998–   )
Star Cruises

First of an impressive pair of stylish large cruise ships, the 75,388-gross-ton *SuperStar Leo*, delivered in September 1998 by Meyer Werft, Papenburg, Germany, is based at Hong Kong, targeted at the growing Oriental cruise market. Her itinerary consists mainly of short cruises to China and Vietnam. Predominantly Eastern in style and flavour, there is also evidence of Western influences in her décor and design features. Likewise, the dining facilities cater for a wide range of regional tastes — Oriental, European and North American. The *SuperStar Leo*'s featured show lounge — the two-level Moulin Rouge — has a revolving stage. A reported possible transfer of the *SuperStar Leo* to associate company Norwegian Cruise Line sometime during the 2001 season will, if it goes ahead, result in a name change to *Norwegian Leo* and reallocation to Hawaii for operation on seven-night cruises.
Bettina Rohrbrecht

Above: The *SuperStar Leo*'s elegant Tivoli Pool and lido area, with its columns and rotundas, hints of Roman baths. *Meyer Werft*

Above right: The high-level Galaxy of Stars observation lounge on Deck 12 can seat 450 passengers. *Meyer Werft*

Right: The Magellan Restaurant, located on Deck 6 of the *SuperStar Leo*. *Meyer Werft*

SuperStar Virgo
(1999-   )
Star Cruises

The *SuperStar Virgo* entered service in August 1999. Like her sister ship *SuperStar Leo*, she is diesel-electric-powered, with twin screws. Her principal dimensions are 879ft (268m) length overall and 105ft (32m) maximum beam.

SuperStar Virgo is based at Singapore, operating short coastal and inter-island cruises of three- to four-night duration around the Malaysian Peninsula. Star Cruises has four even larger vessels under construction — the 91,000-gross-ton *SuperStar Libra* and *SuperStar Scorpio*, and the 112,000-gross-ton *SuperStar Sagittarius II* and *SuperStar Capricorn II* — all due to be commissioned by 2004. Their introduction will increase Star Cruises' total passenger capacity to well in excess of 12,000 berths. *Meyer Werft*

The generous-sized casino aboard the *SuperStar Virgo*. *Meyer Werft*

The *SuperStar Virgo*'s Grand Piazza extends through seven decks — Nos 7 to 13. *Meyer Werft*

Veendam
(1996-   )
Holland-America Line

Completed in May 1996 by Fincantieri, the *Veendam* was the last of the 'Statendam'-class quartet. Décor, layout and furnishings are similar to those of her earlier sisters, as are the names of her public rooms: Rotterdam Restaurant, Crow's Nest Lounge, etc. Lacking the excessive glitz of some modern cruise ships, the *Veendam* is a comfortable, elegant and well-appointed vessel, operating for much of the time in the Caribbean, serving the Premium sector of the cruise market. She is pictured at Venice. *Holland-America Line*

Victoria
(1966-   )
P&O Cruises
(ex-*Sea Princess*, ex-*Kungsholm*)

The elegant and intimate *Victoria*, which exudes old-world tradition and charm, is the former Swedish-flag North Atlantic liner *Kungsholm*, taken over by P&O in 1979 and renamed *Sea Princess*. Sixteen years later, in October 1995, with the passing of the original *Oriana*, she was renamed *Victoria* to bolster the P&O Cruises operation based in Southampton, in recognition of the growing demand for cruises out of the United Kingdom to the Mediterranean and Atlantic islands. Designed for deep-water operation, she suits longer cruises and her programme has included circumnavigations of the globe. The *Victoria*'s two-tiered Coral Restaurant on C Deck has a wealth of 18th-century Chinese porcelain on display. She also has a Princess Theatre and a variety of bars and cafés to suit all tastes. Reports in the trade press have intimated that P&O may dispose of the *Victoria* in the near future as other new ships join the *Oriana*, *Arcadia* and *Aurora*. *P&O Cruises*

Vision of the Seas
(1998-   )
Royal Caribbean International

Last of the 'Project Vision' series, the Chantiers de L'Atlantique-built *Vision of the Seas*, which entered service in May 1998, is seen departing Vancouver. At 78,941 gross tons, and 915ft (279m) overall length, she and her sister *Rhapsody of the Seas* are somewhat larger than the first two ships of the series, the *Legend of the Seas* and *Splendour of the Seas*, whose gross tonnage is 69,130 and overall length 867ft (264m). The *Vision of the Seas'* public rooms include the Windjammer Café — an informal dining area — and a more traditional main restaurant laid out on two decks and overlooking the ocean on two sides. Royal Caribbean International presents the *Vision of the Seas* and her predecessors as floating contemporary-quality hotels conveying guests between the various destinations of their particular cruise programme. *En route* they provide good-quality dining fare and plenty of entertainment options to occupy the guests. *Ian Shiffman*

Volendam
(1999-   )
Holland-America Line

With the exception of the new cruise ship
Amsterdam, the Italian-built *Volendam* and her sister
Zaandam are the latest vessels to join the Holland-
America Line fleet, representing a development in
both size and amenities over the previous
'Statendam'-class ships. Together with the *Rotterdam*
and *Amsterdam*, they represent the culmination of a
16-year building programme; comprising 10 new
purpose-built ships, this has elevated the company to
a position as one of the top operators in the industry,
with a capacity of more than 13,000 berths. Like
many other new ships in recent years, the *Volendam*
made a delayed entry into service (in October 1999),
the hold-up resulting from overloaded capacity at the
Fincantieri yards. This is a graphic measure of the
current high level of demand for new passenger-ship
construction, which only a limited number of
specialist shipyards appear able to handle within the
competitively tight budgets imposed on them by the
operators. Compared to the 'Statendam' class, the
Volendam and *Zaandam* have many more cabins
with private balconies (or 'mini-suites', as the trade
prefers to describe this type of accommodation). The
Volendam has two dining rooms, the main 747-seat
Rotterdam and the intimate 88-seat Marco Polo.
A large crystal-glass sculpture called 'Caleido'
dominates her atrium area. Décor throughout the
ship follows two themes — one floral, the other the
cinema, emphasising Hollywood filmstars and
movies. Now part of the huge Carnival Corporation
group of companies, Holland-America retains its
reputation for high-quality accommodation and
service, established during the company's days as a
prominent North Atlantic route operator.
Holland-America Line

Voyager of the Seas
(1999-   )
Royal Caribbean International

The largest passenger ship in the world by a huge margin when she entered service in November 1999, the *Voyager of the Seas* is the lead ship of the 'Project Eagle' series, which will ultimately comprise five cruise vessels. These mammoth ships, of quite epic proportions, can truly be described as floating leisure resorts. The *Voyager of the Seas* has public spaces to rival those of any contemporary, competitive cruise ship. They embrace all the typical interior facilities now fitted almost as standard, along with many exciting, ground-breaking features, including the first ice-skating rink to be installed on an ocean-going ship. Based at Miami, serving the Caribbean circuit, the giant *Voyager of the Seas* and, from 2000, the *Explorer of the Seas* dictated the upgrading of the passenger-handling arrangements ashore. A new 250,000sq ft terminal has been commissioned by the Miami Port Authority specially to accommodate the 'Voyager of the Seas'-class ships (each with capacity for 3,840 passengers) and other, future cruise vessels of this immense scale. The *Adventure of the Seas*, third of the class, is scheduled for delivery in April 2002. The 'Project Eagle' ships have diesel-electric engines driving triple 'Azipod' propulsion units.
Royal Caribbean International

Top right: The three-level main restaurant on the *Voyager of the Seas*. The levels (rather than the rooms themselves) have names — Carmen, La Bohème and Magic Flute.
Royal Caribbean International

Centre right: The five-deck-high, 1,350-seat theatre has been styled on and named after the La Scala opera house in Milan.
Royal Caribbean International

Bottom right: The 394ft (120m)-long Royal Promenade, which extends upwards through four decks and is illuminated by natural light from above — an immense open area within the heart of the *Voyager of the Seas*. *Kvaerner Masa*

Right: One of the two Centrum lobbies — something of a contradiction in terms — that rise through 11 decks from the Royal Promenade.
Royal Caribbean International

Below: The Pig & Whistle pub, located on the *Voyager of the Seas'* Royal Promenade.
Kvaerner Masa

Wind Song (1987-   )
Windstar Cruises

One of three similar, modern-style sail cruising ships introduced in the late 1980s, the 5,703-gross-ton Wind Song, like her consorts Wind Star and Wind Spirit, is completely fore-and-aft-rigged on her four sturdy masts. The sails are power-hoisted and adjusted, and their set is computer-controlled. She is seen here underway in Table Bay, Cape Town. The ship's passenger capacity is restricted to 150, the emphasis (as on other sail cruises) being on a relaxing experience rather than on an exotic lifestyle in a setting of grand on-board amenities. Hence, public rooms are limited in number and are on the small side, although the décor and furnishings are of a high standard. There is a plentiful supply of water-sports equipment. The Wind Song and her sisters are operated by Windstar Cruises, a Carnival Corporation concern. A planned fourth ship of the class, the Wind Saga, was never built.
Ian Shiffman

Wind Surf (1990-   )
Windstar Cruises
(ex-*Club Med I*, ex-*Lafayette*)

One of the two largest sail-cruisers ever built, the 14,475-gross-ton *Wind Surf* entered service for Club Med Cruises in February 1990 and was acquired by Windstar Cruises in March 1998. Her sister ship, the *Club Med II*, is still with her former owners. Pictured moored at Lisbon, the *Wind Surf* measures 614ft (187m) in overall length, exceeding the size of many engine-propelled cruise ships. Her five masts support a total sail area of 26,880sq ft (2,500sq m), all of which is managed without manual intervention. As with the smaller ships of the 'Wind Star' type, the sails are controlled electronically by the use of computers located on the navigation bridge. There is accommodation for a maximum of 312 passengers and, surprisingly, on a vessel of this character, reasonably good provision of passenger amenities. The main restaurant, seating 272, is complemented by a small Verandah Bistro. During a major refit in May 1998, the health spa and fitness centre were totally renovated and now constitute one of the ship's principal facilities. The *Wind Surf* and her sister, along with the three ships of the 'Wind Star' group, were constructed at Ateliers et Chantiers du Havre. *Ian Shiffman*

Zaandam (2000-   )
Holland-America Line

Sister ship to the *Volendam*, the *Zaandam* was commissioned in February 2000. At 60,906 gross tons, she measures 777ft (237m) in length, and has berths for 1,824 passengers. Like all recently-completed Holland-America cruise ships she was built by Fincantieri in Italy. Her engines are diesel-electric, having a total power output of 50,287hp (37,500kW) and driving twin controllable-pitch screw propellers. Comparable with the *Volendam* in her appointments, her interior layout follows a similar pattern and her décor and furnishings are to the same high standard. The *Zaandam* is a stylish ship with a relaxed atmosphere, offering her passengers a comprehensive range of dining, entertainment, leisure and exercise facilities.
Holland-America Line

The *Zaandam*'s Seaview Lounge. The main theme of the ship's décor, extending through many public areas, is musical instruments and memorabilia.
Holland-America Line

Zenith (1992-   )
Celebrity Cruises

The second ship of its type, the *Zenith* joined the *Horizon* in April 1992. Broadly similar, in terms of the range and layout of their accommodation, these ships offer a premium product for the discerning traveller and represent good value for money. They are comfortable, stylish and reasonably spacious for vessels of their size. Like the *Horizon*, the *Zenith* was built at Papenburg by Meyer Werft. She measures 47,255 gross tons and 682ft (208m) in overall length. *Royal Caribbean International*

The *Zenith*'s Caravelle Restaurant, with raised central section. *Royal Caribbean International*

The *Zenith*'s two-level show lounge, located off a double-width indoor promenade. *Royal Caribbean International*

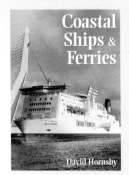